The Changing Face of London Road South.

Then and Now.

By C. L. Hook

2

ISBN 978-0-9934031-7-0

Published by The Old Beach Company Press, 2019

Special thanks to The Robert Whybrow Collection, Peter Jenkins, Archant, Ian Robb, Jack Rose Society, Lowestoft Heritage Centre, British Newspaper Archive, Lowestoft Records Office, The John Holmes Collection, Bert Collyer, David Van Zandt, Marina Knight and all the shop Keepers who donated an old picture of their shops in the writing of this book.

 All attempts have been made to contact copyright owners and I apologise if I've missed anybody off the above list.

Please don't forget to check out our other titles.

Lowestoft's pubs, Beerhouses, Taverns, Inns & Stores, Then & Now.

Lowestoft High Street, The Butcher, the Baker and the candlestick Maker.

The Changing Face of London Road North, Then & Now.

Robert W Hook, A Forgotten Local Hero.

The Hook & Pask Mysteries. The Curse of the Hooded Monk / The Vengeful Ten/ The Case of the Carbuncled Ruby.

Book printed by www.bookprintinguk.com

Front cover: Multiview's of London Road South.

Rear cover: View down London Rd South.

NEW PLAYHOUSE THEATRE

LOWESTOFT

Box Office 9.30 a.m. to 9.30 p.m.   Telephone : 1102

REPERTORY AT ITS BEST !

Week Commencing **Mon., November 20th, 1950**

Nightly at 7.30

THE EAST ANGLIAN REPERTORY COMPANY present

LET NOTHING YOU DISMAY

A CHRISTMAS PLAY FOR OLD AND YOUNG ALIKE

By Alan Broadhurst

Seats available Mon., Tues., Wed. and Fri. Evenings for Children under 14 years at 1/- each to all parts.

Matinee Sat., Nov. 25th, at 2.30 p.m.   All seats at 1/- each

Foreword

In recent years London Road South and South Lowestoft in general has been described as the poor relation of London Road North, full of second-hand shops and charity shops. In fact, London Road South has been the victim, the same as London Road North and the whole of the country, of the increasing use of online shopping as people seem to find it easier than trying to find a parking space or venture out into these areas of town.

I'm hoping that you're sitting down reading this book about London Road South and that you didn't buy it online but rather ventured out into this big bold world. I'm hoping you went to Waterstones or one of the other local book shops, oh yes, we don't have any, anymore. It's all moved online. It doesn't matter either way because what counts is your reading it.

London Road South was once made up of all the shops you would find on the local High Street, they had their own stationers, butchers quite a few pubs, dairies, tobacconists, a couple of cinemas, a swimming pool and fancy drapers, whatever they were?

It seemed when Lowestoft received heavy bombing during the Second World War that the businesses which were bombed out in London Road North and the High Street simply packed up what they could salvage and trampled across the bridge to London Road South. These were mainly Boots and Woolworths, to name a few. They found an empty shop and stayed well into the 1950's before upping sticks and moving back to London Road North.

I didn't know whether in writing this book to include Pier Terrace because it seemed strange that the odd number starts at 39 and the evens at 136. But 136 has now gone because when the petrol station sat on the now KFC site it was its number and now in 2018 the KFC has adopted the address of Marine Parade, so the even numbers now start at 138.

Back in 1892 the numbers start at Pier Terrace with No.1 nearest the bridge and then running down that side of the street to Kirkley to No.120 and then across the road back to the now KFC site but not in numbers but rather houses turned into shops all with house names like Venlaw Cottages, Echam Villas, South Cliff Villas, Kirkley Villas, Waveney Villas etc. Maybe Peto was planning to build behind his fine terrace of Marine Parade? We will never know.

This book is dedicated to the memory

of past and present residents of

London Road South.

Saint John's Church.

In 1853 at the cost of Sir Morton Peto the Lucas Brothers started work on John Louth Clemence design for the church. His vision for the church included a hagioscope into the pier of the north transept and chancel arches to allow the congregation there to see the pulpit and reading desk. Peto gave the church as a gift to the growing town to provide a place of worship for the locals and visitors alike. In the background between No.39 and the church you can just make out the Saint John's School.

During the Second World War the spire gave the War Office a bit of a problem as it was a landmark which gave the Germans something to identify the town and all attempts to camouflage it with canvas failed when the strong East coast winds blew it away. The clock seen in the picture wasn't added to the spire until 1897 and eighty years on it came down when work started in December 1977 to demolish it. Being close to the North Sea the salt air and spray didn't mix well with the Lucas Brothers choice of using soft stone to build it as it started to crumble with the floods of 1953 not helping with the brick works decay. At the time of demolishment, the local heritage and archaeological society wanted to purchase it but were too late as the contractor had already sold it to a collector from Solihull. Not too sure on the pictures age but it must be around the 1930's, you can see the tram cable post is being used as a lamp post.

No.39, London Road South.

As you can see if you closely compare the two pictures of No.39 over the years a lot of updating of the building has been undertaken. It appears to have had a fireplace removed as the chimney stack has been removed, in addition another bay window on the left-hand side and above both on each side of the frontage. Today in 2018 the building is called Hevingham House and until recently the home of a firm of Architects, but back in 1892 the house was recorded as St Johns Vicarage and was a smaller building and between then and the time the picture was taken on the right it was knocked down and replaced with Hevingham House. The Vicarage was occupied back in 1892 by the Reverend B Innes.

No.41, London Road South.

NEW PLAYHOUSE THEATRE

LOWESTOFT

Box Office 9.30 a.m. to 9.30 p.m.   Telephone : 1102

REPERTORY AT ITS BEST !

Week Commencing **Mon., November 20th, 1950**

Nightly at 7.30

THE EAST ANGLIAN REPERTORY COMPANY present

LET NOTHING YOU DISMAY

A CHRISTMAS PLAY FOR OLD AND YOUNG ALIKE

By Alan Broadhurst

Seats available Mon., Tues., Wed. and Fri. Evenings for Children under 14 years at 1/- each to all parts.

Matinee Sat., Nov. 25th, at 2.30 p.m.   All seats at **1/-** each

In 1892 there was a terrace of houses on the plot the cinema now stands and then it was rebuilt into an auctioneers sales room sometime around 1910. In the 1925 kelly's Directory, it looks like Mr. F. C. Symond had turned his once thriving business from a sales room to a roller-skating rink and by the next time it appears in the phone book it had changed use again with Mr. Symonds turning it into the Playhouse Cinema. By the late 1940's the cinema had gone through another metamorphosis and had become The New Playhouse Theatre and as the newspaper advert says it was repertory theatre at its best. In the 1950's after the theatre had been re-named the Arcadia Theatre it played host to a young Michael Caine and at the age of 21, he stayed in the town for a year and met his first wife. Whilst in Lowestoft at the Arcadia theatre (with Jackson Stanley's players) he appeared in nine plays. After the Arcadia the theatre was re-branded the Theatre Royal and when that failed it became the Theatre Royal Bingo Club and then the Coronet Social Club up to 1989 when it became the Hollywood cinema and today the East Coast Cinema.

No.43, London Road South.

No.43 would be the building nearest to the left of the picture and disappeared sometime in the 1960 as telephone listing for the building only go up to 1957.

Listed in 1922 to the mid 1950's it was the home of Powell & Co who operated out of the building as printers, but in 1925 in addition to Powell, Lowestoft Guild of Arts & Crafts were also based in the building.

From the 1950's on it was the home of C & S Electrical Ltd and their advert in the phone book read; Soames & K. C. Mullard. Radio & Television Sales & service. Non-price ring battery specialists; electrical, installations-domestic & industrial Tel: 1682.

No.45, London Road South.

In 1922 D. Leighton & Son ran their building contractors and decorating business from the address. In 1948-49 the business appears to have gone and his wife is running the building as Mrs Leighton boarding house, but that was short lived as by 1952 to the late 1970's it became Mrs F Chipperfield boarding house. I always remember this building for a long time being a diving business called Learn Scuba, but in the flood of 2013 when Lowestoft had a large tidal surge it caused £80,000 worth of stock damage to the store and it relocated. After the building had been renovated Deerheart Collective moved in offering bespoke tattooing, laser treatments and barbering services.

No.49-51, London Road South.

In 1892 No.49 was No.13 and the home of a Mr F. J. Rix who traded as a sanitary plumber. Moving on to 1925 Francis Joseph Rix had changed his occupation to a decorator. By 1934 Daniel Jason Woolston had moved in and his occupation was a photographer and by the 1950's the building was the home of Lowestoft Hosiery Repair Company (nylon, silk & rayon speedily repaired). I remember it as the London & Manchester Assurance Company as grandad took out a policy for me when I turned ten.

Moving on to No.51 and it was No.14 in 1892 and it was the home of Miss Anne Walker, a teacher of the pianoforte. In the 1909 Kelly Directory she was listed as a professor of music and remained in the house until the 1930's when a Mr Cecil Cubitt moved in. Mr Cubitt was an antique dealer and stayed in the house until the 1940's when a Mrs G Guymer moved in and started a ladies hairdressers but not after the frontage was changed to a shop frontage. After she left it continued to be a hairdressers but now under the ownership of a Mrs Mary Jackson and by the 1970's Michael Blowers was operating as the Royal Salon ladies hairdressers. Today in 2018 both shops have been returned to private houses.

No.61, London Road South.

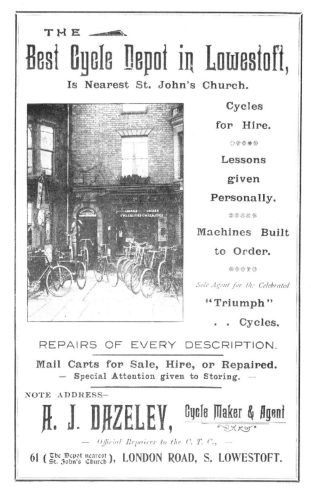

In 1892 No.61 was Mrs. W. Porter's fancy goods store until Mr. A. J. Dazeley opened up shop as a cycle maker & agent for triumph cycle. His tag line was that he was the nearest bike shop to St Johns Church. In 1909 Mr. Dazeley was gone and a Mr Perry John Gibbons had taken only the bike shop until the 1920's when it became a confectioner under the ownership of George Munnings.

From the 1920's to the 1970's the shop as a confectioners had many different owners, James Francis in 1925, Mrs Richardson in 1938 and lastly George Cowles. In the Kelly listing for 1972 the shop was still owned by the Cowles family, but it had passed to his son, a Mr. R. E. Cowles who with his business partner P. R. Foyster opened up a newsagents which stayed open well into the late 1990's. Today in 2019 the building is in a shocking state and is up for sale again, so its future is uncertain.

No.63-65, London Road South.

Before the terrace was torn down, No.63 and 65 were both separate buildings until sometime in the late 1960's when the unit we see today was built. In 1862 No.63 was a boarding house run by a Mrs Widdows and No.65 was the business of Mr. G. F. Simnett who was a china & glass dealer along with being a coal merchant. In the 1920's No.63 was the offices of David Wilson who ran his insurance business from the address and then appears to be a private house until the 1970's when it was taken over by the business at No.65 which was Centre Garage run by a Mr. B. R. Ibberson who was a Bedford & Vauxhall dealer.

Moving on to No.65 after 1892 Mrs Widdows continued to have her boarding house until the 1920's when it became a newsagents run by a Mr Eric White and then in 1934 the newsagents had been replaced with Mr Allan Disney grocers and confectionery business. In 1938 the building became Ibberson garage and it continued as a garage right into the 1980's, I remember the building as being Kenny Cantor Theatre School but now it's Mandarin Cycles, the only place south side of the bridge you can get a bike, I think?

No. 67-77, London Road South.

In 1892 all the above space was made up of a terrace of five houses with the exception of No.67-77 who in the 1920's was the home of Percy John Gibbons cycle shop which was then taken over by Mr R. Wright in the 1930's who then carried on in the cycles business until the 1970's when he switched to cars. In the meantime No.75-77 in the 1940's became Langford Garage and then in the late 1950's Mann-Egerton & Co took over the site. Today in 2018 the site is CMV Automotive dealing with the sale of classic, performance and prestige cars.

No.87-89, London Road South.

No.79 to No.85 has spent their entire life as private houses and it is not until you reach No.87 until you reach a number which has been a shop all its life.

No.87 started off in 1892 as a private house and was the home of a Mr. Cunningham but by 1909 Mr Dazeley who did have his cycle shop at No.61 had moved to this location until the 1920's. In and around 1920 the shop switched from bikes to cabbages and became Mrs Florence Ward's grocers shop until in the 1934 Kelly directory it is listed as Mrs Elizabeth Garwood's greengrocers.

Once the greengrocers had gone the shop was taken over by a Mr J. E. Rosenburg who operated it as a jeweller and watch dealer until the 1950's when Sheppard and Rackham had taken over as jewellers and to this day it is Gage.

No.89 has always been a private house and in 1892 Mrs Tooke is listed as a costumier at the address. In 1909 the house had become Mrs Bell's Lodging House but in 1922 the house had changed ownership to a Mr Earl Hipworth who's occupation was recorded as a tailor. Hipworth stayed well into the 1950's until Mr Leonard Barnard moved in and today in 2019 it's the offices of Gage Estate Agents.

No.91-93, London Road South.

No.91 (Minerva Terrace) in 1892 was the home of Mr. R. W. Massingham but by 1909 it had become John Saunders lodging house. In 1922 Alec Cannell moved in and then after until the 1960's it was the home of Ivan Herbert Doy and today in 2018 it makes up Gage estate agents.

No.93 has gone just like the rest of the terrace which stretched once to Mill Road, but No.93 started out in 1892 as the home of Mr & Mrs Bryant. She was a Staymaker and he was a plasterer. In 1909 the building was Mrs Leaks apartments and sometime around the mid 1930's a shop frontage was placed onto it becoming Daniel fraser fruiters. As you can see from the advent it became a gift shop which was run by a Mrs Weed, this was around the 1950's until it was pulled down for the expanding Mann Egerton garage.

No.95-109, London Road South.

VISIT:— **SYDS** Tel. 3232

TROPICAL FISH and AQUARIUMS — FERTILIZERS/GRASS SEEDS
AND ALL GARDEN SUNDRIES — BULK ORDERS DELIVERED
THROUGHOUT LOWESTOFT

Pet Shop and Garden Centre, 103 London Rd. South, Lowestoft

No.95 in 1892 was a lodging house run by Mrs Mobbs and continued until it was pulled down as a private house. No.97 to 101 were the same too, all private houses and it wasn't until you arrive at No.103 you find another shop. In 1922 it was the home of Albert Harry Coleman and listed in 1938 one of my family members a Mr Walter Hook had the building separated into apartments. As you can see by the above advert in the 1960's-70's Sydney E Prentice operated his shop Syds Pet-Food & Garden Centre. The next shop you come across is No.109, it started off as a private house and the first business at the address belonged to David Ellis Leighton who operated as a builder and undertaker. The next business was around the 1920s and was an artificial tooth manufacturer which by 1938 was replaced by Lowestoft foot clinic-orthopaedic, consultant and chiropodist. All this terrace would be gone by the 1970's and replaced with the rapidly expanding Mann Egerton & Co motor engineers which started at No.97-99 in the 1920's. Long gone now in 2019 Mann Egerton has been replaced with another dealership.

No.109a, London Road South.

In 1892 to give it it's full name Carlton House was a grocers and wine merchants run by B. G. Beaumont. In 1909 the building had changed its name to Lowestoft South Hall and was now the home of Mrs L. Rose's milliner shop (hat maker). By the 1920s the milliner business had passed to a Mrs Jennie Craven but not for long as by the mid 1920's the whole ground floor had become Josiah. J. Smiths motor show room with the Lowestoft South Hall above.

Listed in the 1934 Kelly Directory the building had been taken over by Collins and Smith, I'm not too sure if this was the same Smith from the previous car business? But they set up shop as wireless and electrical contractors. After the Second World War the building was taken over by Percy Wigg who used the ground floor as his furnisher showroom and carried on well into the 1960's. Over the last couple of decades the building has seen quite a few changes but for most of that time it's been a few different restaurants and today in 2019 it's the fortune Cookie Chinese restaurant, oh and it's lost the a off 109.

No.121, London Road South.

121 DRAKE'S,
confectioners, tobacconists, groceries, &c (open 7 days a week; 8 am -9 pm)

In 1909 No.121 was listed as a private house and Mrs Rix lived at the address right up to the mid 1920's.

Sometime in the early 1930's the building was converted into the shop we see today and had become by 1934 a confectioners owned and run by a Mrs Annie Parr. By 1938 the confectioners were taken over by a Mr Donald Davey who carried it on as the same business. After the Second World War the shop became Eastern Counties Home Service whos main business was carpet cleaning. In 1950 the shop was taken over again and became Miss H. J. Allison wool shop but by 1957 the shop had become Baby Land who traded also as a wool shop. By the time the shop appears in the Kelly Directory it had become as above, Drakes confectioners, tobacconist and grocers. Today in 2019 the shop is along the same theme being a Newsagents, General Stores and Off Licence.

No.127, London Road South.

In 1909 the building was the home of Riches Nockold who ran his business as a furniture dealer and in 1922 the building started its association with hardware when the Midland Hardware Company moved in. By the 1930's the shop was Prince Arthur Hipperson's Hardware Shop which after the Second World war the business had passed to firstly S. J. Dicken and then a few years later to K. J. Dicken right up to the 1980's. I always remember it until it was converted into flats as The Dog Shop, which was funny enough a pet shop, the only one at that time on London Road South.

No.133, London Road South.

There's not much to say about this building and this shop on London Road South as from since it was built it stayed as the same type of business right up to the 1980's. The building first started out its journey under the ownership of Youngman-Preston Brewers as an off licence. By the 1920's it was under the ownership of E. Lacon & Co and finished off in the 80's as a Whitbread & Co store. When I was a child, dad purchased me my first computer which was a Commodore 16 and after a year of enjoyment it buggered up! So, we took it to R. A. Electronics who was run by a retired navy man and within a few minutes he fixed it. Since then the shop has really just been a succession of second-hand shops but I do think it has beautiful window frames. Today in 2019 it is run as a secondhand shop by the Alfies Organisation.

No.141, London Road South.

REGENCY SALON

TOP HAIRSTYLISTS and WIGMAKERS

141 LONDON ROAD SOUTH, LOWESTOFT 3410

P.P. Mr. David (Top Hairstylist)

In 1909 Frederick Robert Welchman worked from the house running his solicitors practice before the shop was added before the Second World War. After that it spent most of its life as a ladies hairdressers first by a Mrs Nora Edwards before becoming Regency Salon as can be seen above. I can always remember this shop being one of the only three Laundromats in this town when I think today, we are down to two remaining laundromats. One is in the high street and the other is on westwood avenue, but now the Laundromat has been replaced with Gateway to Hope.

Gateway to Hope provides a safe place for the homeless or otherwise troubled people who can drop in to talk with a volunteer member.

No.143, London Road South.

The same as No.141 the building started out as a private house and it wasn't really used as a shop until around 1909 when it was listed as Arthur Sullivan's Confectioner shop. From the 1920's onwards it began its long association with being an opticians.

In 1934 the shop was owned by F. J. Parker-sight testing opticians and from the 1940's onwards right up to the 1960's and the owner then was a Mr. F. E. Field. In the 1970's the shop had passed to a Mr. W. J. Sabell.

It's been a selection of different types of businesses since then and before it was Beauty Matters it was Skin Graphics.

No.145, London Road South.

In 1909 the building was listed as Mr. E. C. Semitt, provisions merchants store while upstairs in the main house a Dr William Palmer was living and in the phone book he was listed as a physician and surgeon. After he left in the 1930's it became Kenmare and as you can see in the advert above it was described as comfortable and homely, not sure what all amusements? But at least it was one minute from the sea.

From the 1970's on it became the home downstairs as Health Stores selling a full range of health foods. Up to 2018 it was the home of Ralphs, I did buy a washing machine off him once and Kenmare is long gone! Today in 2019 its been replaced with Alfies Organisation which supports families with Autism and ADHD.

No.147, London Road South.

In 1909 this building was the offices of the Lowestoft Weekly Press-Norfolk News-Eastern Daily Press & the Eastern Evening News. But by the 1920's this building began its long association with being a second-hand shop and furniture dealer.

The first man in there was Arthur Betts in 1922 and he was followed by Henry Colebrook in 1938. Next came Douglas Morgan who was then replaced in the 1960's by Home Services who first started off as furniture dealers and by the 70's as second-hand dealers. It's now the Lowestoft BBQ centre.

No.149, London Road South.

BOMBARDMENT OF LOWESTOFT, APRIL 25TH 1916.
LONDON ROAD SOUTH.

In 1892 the building was the home to a grocers run by a Mr. A. Adams but by 1909 Mr. Edgar & Co had moved in and was operating as a photographer. On the 25th April 1916 Lowestoft was under bombardment by the German Navy and the damage can been seen inflicted to Mr Edgar's shop on the left. After it was rebuilt, he soldiered on for a few years, but by the 1920's Mrs Emily Gosling had opened the shop to sell pastries. In the 1930's Albert McMinns took over selling leather goods followed my Herbert Beckett, but he needed more space and took over No.151 as well. Recently it was Ralph Gennery used furniture, but today its become Dr Johnson's Coffee Shoppe.

No.153, London Road South.

In 1892 No.153 was the home of F Hannant, stationers. In 1909 Frank Hannant stationers was now a fancy repository and by 1922 it was a library & bazaar. Moving on to the 1930's and it was more like the Hannants I remember in London Road North, wool and toy shop.

After the Second World War, Wards Restaurant opened at the address but by the 1950's it was taken over by a Mr Kalinowski. In the 1970's it was Town Grills Restaurant. In 2017 when I took this picture the shop was Titan Computers and before that Di-Lusso, womens boutique/ fashion shop. In 2019 it is a shop called Seagulls & Other Birds.

No.155, London road South.

In 1892 the shop was Johnson & Co who ran it as a Pianoforte Warehouse, but by 1909 a Mr. S. A. Reffell had took over the shop and was operating as ironmongers & electric bell fitters. In 1922 the ironmongers were owned by Mr William Reffel but in a short time Hannants next door had moved in. By 1938 the shop had changed use again and this time into a grocers run by Michael Mancini. In the 1940's Hughes had moved in and were trading as electrical engineers, but by the 50's P. W. Poole had moved in and started selling flowers & fruit.

In the 1970's the shop had become Abbey Potteries and was listed in the phone book as china dealers. Since then it's had many uses, I can remember it as a bike shop but today it's a Game exchange with those more retro games. I've been in there myself buying dvd's, check out their Facebook page if you get a second.

No.157-159, London Road South.

In 1909 Kirkley Hall was split into two stores No.157 was the home of R. T. Hayes who traded as a milliner and next door at No.159 Small & Co operated as tailors. In 1916 at the time of the Lowestoft bombardment no damage was caused to the building which was such a relief to Reffell & Co who had converted the building from two stores into one big unit. From the 1920's Brett & Sons had moved in selling house furnishings and china. During the Second World War Woolworths in London Rd North was totally destroyed and relocated to the shop in London Rd South right up to the 1950's while the old store was rebuilt. In the 50's Woolworths moved back north and Lowestoft Co-operative Society Ltd moved in and set up shop as outfitters. In the 1970's Jewsons moved in and the building became a builders merchants with Jewsons having their main sawmill in Belvedere Road. As you can see in 2019 Parkers is in residence dealing in formal wear and formal hire.

No.161, London Road South.

 In 1909 George Durrant & Son operated out of the building as a green grocers after moving from over the road at No.156a some years earlier. On the morning of the 24th April 1916 it started out as a normal day until the German Navy started to shell the town, but nevertheless Durrant rebuilt and carried on in the address until the late 1920's when Isidoro Capaldi opened as a confectioner. The shop had R. Atherton operating out of it up to the mid 50's and that was when the Midland Bank moved in and started taking the money from the residents and businesses on London Road South. It's been so many different shops since the bank moved out, an antique shop, computer shop, property management shop and now Klash Photography. It says on the signage "Having a baby is such a precious time in our lives, make sure you capture it!"

No.167, London Road South.

In 1909 J Brett & Sons, Complete Home Furnishers were operating from the building, but at the time of the Lowestoft bombardment the shop was open as a provision merchants. If you remember by the 1920's Brett & Sons moved into Kirkley Hall at No.157-159 and it wasn't until the 1920's the building was occupied again and this time by Frederick Norton & Son's, who were tobacconists. In the 1950's Norman J Brundle moved in and set up shop as radio engineers and dealers, but by 1957 the shop became Hughes. By the 1970's Sarah Edith had moved in and was trading as an antiques dealer. Before moving last year further up the street Windsor Gallery was trading at the address but now in 2019 it is the new home of Eventopia. On their Facebook page it is described as a Fairytale Boutique, children's parties, princess hire, balloons, sweets, chair covers and event and wedding planning.

No.169, London Road North.

In 1892 a Mr S Money was running his watchmaking & jewellers from the address, but by 1909 Ernest Ward was operating out of the building as a watchmaker. By the 1920's the business in the building had switched to a tailors & outfitters run by Mortimer Stanley Brundle who carried on well into the 1960's. Up to last year the shop was the home of Floral Passion, but now in 2019 it is The Magpie Moment.

No.171, London Road South.

As you can see in the advert from the 1880's the shop started out its career as Webb's Kirkley Stores and you can see from the advert they sold quite a collection of goods. Next in 1909 the shop was then operating as a drapers run by A. Smerdon. He carried on into the 1920's when Mortimer Stanley Brundle expanded his tailors and outfitters into the shop. In late 1930's the shop began its long association with hairdressing when W. G. Powell moved in offering Service and Satisfaction. In the 1972 Kelly directory Robert Owen is first listed at the address as a ladies hairdressers and today in 2019 he is still open.

No.173, London Road South.

Fred Norton's Tobacco

WELL KNOWN far and wide for the Large and Excellent Stock always on hand of all kinds of Fancy and Loose Tobaccos. comprising -- Packets and Tins of all sizes, by the leading Tobacco and Cigar Factors of the British Isles, North, South, East and West. Stephen Mitchell and F. & J. Smith's Wonderful Glasgow Smoking Mixtures, W. D. & H. O. Wills', Lambert & Butler's Bird's Eye, Player's Navy Cut, Ogden's, Godfrey Phillips' (B.D.V.), Clarke's (Carlton), Hignett's, Cope's, Murray's, Lloyd's, Brankston's, Gallaher's, including the best of the American productions, such as Old Judge, Old Gold, Old Rip; also Trecker (Boer) from the Transvaal, Craven Mixture (invented by the Earl of Craven), Pioneer, Log Cabin, Four Seasons, and in fact all are of the very highest merit to select from, not forgetting the Working Standard and Imperial Shag at 3d. per oz., without doubt the best value in the trade, same article sold in London and other large centres at 4d. per oz.

In 1892 the shop was a land agent run by Percy Victor Huckle and not so long after Frederick Norton opened up shop as a tobacconist. By the 1920's the now unhealthy smoking habit had been replaced by a sports outfitters call H. R. Moll's Sports House. By the 1930's the name of the shop had changed to Randall Sports, but was still run by the Moll family. After the Second World War the shop had become the Bird Rd Café, but not long after in the 1950's it had become the Kit Kat Kafé.

Jumping to the 1970's, in the 1972 Kelly directory had listed; Unit wise, house furnishers (white wood specialists) I suppose that means white melamine chipboard which was the in thing in wood back then. Today in 2019 Art Eternal Tattoo Studio has moved and its now the home of Market pets.

No.175, London Road South.

In 1892 the building was still a private house and it didn't have its shop frontage added at that point, but in 1909 M. S & Co had opened a store at the address and was operating as a hosiers (a person who sold stockings).

In the 1920's a Herbert Randall set up shop as a confectioner and survived at the location well into the 1940's when the store became Kirkley fruit stores. Peter Beamish carried on selling fruit at No.175 to well into the 1970's when the shop changed again from fruit to clothing when Durrent outfitters moved in.

Today in 2019 the building is for sale but before it was closed it was the Mr. Bumble's Café. It you look on the estate agents web site you'll see the café boasts a 32-seating capacity restaurant, a three-bedroom flat, three room basement, rear garden and sea views and all for the price of £175,000.

Today if you look through the window all you will see is a collection of second-hand goods for sale. Hopefully it will be sold soon and maybe reopen as a café or something else?

No.177, London Road South.

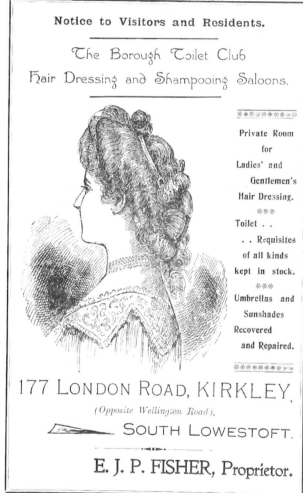

In the 1890's the shop was described in their advert as The Borough Toilet Club, Hair Dressing and Shampooing Saloons. In 1922 a Mr. G. Herbert had moved in and had set up shop as a confectioner and his store and business was that he took over next door, No.179. By 1925 Alfred George Cutts had replaced him as a fruitier and by the time the 1934 Kelly Directory was published, he had expanded his business and he had added florist and greengrocer to his job title. After the Second World War the shop was taken over by a W. B. Cooper who specialised in glasswares. By the time the 1972 Kelly's Directory came out the shop had changed again to Unicolour which was a tv dealer. Today in 2019 it's the Howards Tea Rooms.

No.179, London Road North.

E. H. WALLER,

Baker, Pastrycook, &

and Confectioner,

"Princess .·. Cafe,"

✻ ✻ 179, London Road,
South Lowestoft. .

LIGHT REFRESHMENTS.
HOT AND COLD LUNCHEONS.
TEAS AND SUPPERS.

Awarded Gold Medal Diploma for . . .

Hovis Bread, Scones & Gingerbread.

Bread, Pastry and Cakes,
. . . DELIVERED DAILY.

Bride and Birthday Cakes, made to Order.

From this advert from the 1890's E. H. Waller had their shop in the location and were bakers, pastrycooks, confectioners. With Waller opening up the building as a bakers it started the buildings long association with bread.

By the 1920's Herbert New had taken over the business and was advertised as a confectioner, but from the mid 1920's on, right up to the 1980's Matthes Ltd was there.

Since then the shop has been the Kirkley Village Press, The Attick-Antiques and Academy Clothing. In 2019 it is Bodhi Tree and if you look at the shops Facebook page its described as follows; Fair trade & Ethically sourced shopping haven. Beautiful Women's & Men's clothes, Scarves, Wall hangings, Throws, Cushions, Bags, Jewellery, Incense and more!

No.181-183, London Road South.

In 1892 before it was rebuilt into the monster of a building it is today it was the home of a Mrs Corbyn who traded as a fancy draper.

Once it was rebuilt in 1909 the National Provincial Bank of England was there but by the 1920's it had been renamed as The National Provincial & Union Bank.

The merger in 1968 with Westminster bank surprised the British public & bank community & so ended the National Provincial. The enlarged entity now had a network of 3600 branches. Today in 2018 with the rise of online banking the Natwest has 1600 Branches.

Since the bank went the building has had many uses but today its Lavender House, Aromatherapy, Structural Yoga with energy flow & nutritional clinic. A full range of alternative therapies.

No.185, London Road South.

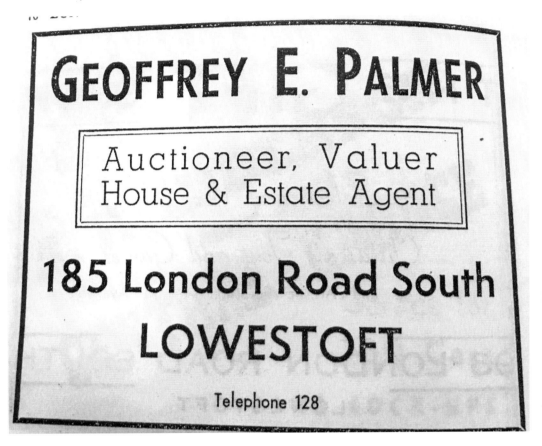

GEOFFREY E. PALMER

Auctioneer, Valuer
House & Estate Agent

185 London Road South
LOWESTOFT

Telephone 128

In 1892 the building number was No.79 London Road South and was the home of a tobacconist run by F. Leach. Moving on 1909 a Mr. J. R. O'Driscoll had taken over the tobacconist and carried on to the 1930's when a Miss C Buck took over. After the Second World War Geoffrey E. Palmer moved in and carried on his business as an Auctioneer, Valuer and House-Estate Agent. In the 1972 Kelly's a Mr. H. W. Wilson had moved in and was selling cooked meats, but in 2019 it is the home of Cheveux Boutique, a Tigi colour salon, hair extensions and make-up.

No.187, London Road South.

In 1892 the number of the building was No.80 and was the business of Turner & Gearing who were fish merchants. By 1909 Turner was long gone and the business was just simply George Gearing but by the 1920's F- Ruthen had taken over the fishmongers. In 1925 the business had switched from fish to meat when Bayfield & Cullen set up shop running their butchers shop from No.187. Only a few years later H. W. Wilson had taken over and stayed well into the 1980's. Since then it has a many new owners one being the Salvation Army who ran the shop as Sally Ann's charity shop. When the picture was taken on the left in 2016 it simply said pharmacy above the door when weeks before it was a Well's Pharmacy. Today in 2019 it now JHOOTS Pharmacy.

No.189, London Road South.

In 1892 No.189 was originally called Kier House and was the home of a Mr. S. Money, watchmaker & Jewellers as well as having another shop is London Road North. By 1909 the shop had changed its use to a bootmakers run by a Mrs Morson and not shortly after that Cooper & Co moved in running the shop as a saddlers. Once the 1930's rolled in the motor car had taken over the road and they switched to high class leather goods. The about picture shows 189 when Desmond was in residence and it looks like the Queen & Prince Philip opened his shop? Today in 2019 Yonney Barber, Gentleman's Hair Salon is operating from the address. Why not pop in for a haircut?

No.191, London Road North.

Back in 1892 the building was Ampthill House and was a dairy owned and run by G. Gibbs who owned it up to 1909 when it came into the ownership of Edward Thomas Cook. Listed in Kelly's in 1948/49 the shop had become C. C. Giles artist materials shop and he carried on well into the 1950's, when in 1957 he switched from paints to chocolate with changing the shop to a confectioners.

In the phone directory for 1972 the shop had become Roy's Fishing Tackle and as a boy my dad took me in there to buy tackle and my maggots for fishing, he traded up to 1998. Today in 2019 the shop has been gutted and completely cleaned up and awaiting a new tenant.

No.193, London Road South.

In 1892 the building had the name of Ely House and was the home of a stationers owned and run by a G. Gwyn.

Moving on to 1909 and the shop had passed to Clifford Norville, in his advert for the local paper it read; Clifford Norville-Music Warehouse (Specializing in tuning and repair of pianos, agents for Chappell gramophones and records, sheet music and instruments.)

Clifford carried on in the address to the mid 1930's when the shop then became, On the Square Library Ltd. On the Square lasted right into the 1950's when in 1952 listed in the phone book the shop had become George Dunworth Tobacconist, but it didn't last more than a few years because shortly after it had become Lavender Laundry- dry cleaners from 1956 to the late 1970's.

Since then it's been many different types of shops, company house has an Iqra Muslim Centre at the address from 2012 to 2017 but I always remember it as a takeaway in one way or another.

No.195, London Road South.

The first time the pub comes up in the White's Directory is the 1840's, were the landlord is a Mrs Charlotte Nicker back when it was the Royal Oak Hotel. Located on London Road South it is a stone's throw from the beach and is still very popular with the inhabitants of Kirkley. You can still see the painted over hotel part of the sign over the front door of the pub, I particularly like the image of the green man surrounded by oak leaves carved into the supports for the bay window above. Why not pop in for a pint?

No.203, London Road South.

 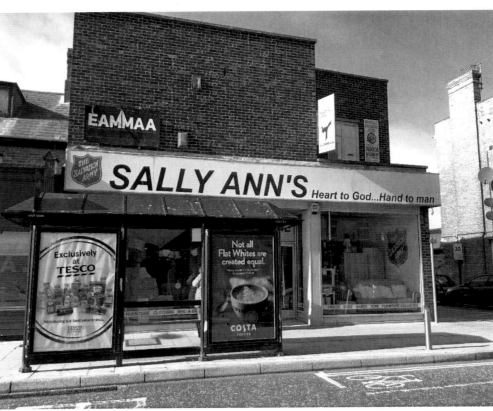

 Located on the corner of Clifton Road the Red Lion was next door to the Royal Oak, it was first numbered No.84 London Road South and then in 1900 the street was re-numbered, and it became 201-203 London Road South. In 1937 it was renamed the Lion Hotel due to the one in the High Street having closed and the name being available. In the late 1960's the landlord called time and the hotel was demolished to make way for a purpose-built Lipton's store, since then a few other business moved in, mostly furniture stores due to the space the store offered but now is 2019 it is still the home of the Salvation Army's furniture sales with a martial arts studio above.

No.205, London Road South.

 In 1892 the shop was numbered No.86 and was the home of Mr. J. Balls who was a butcher, this started this shops long association with being a butchers shop. Next to move in around 1909 was James Nelson & Sons, who also were butchers. By the 1920's the British and Argentine Meat Co Ltd had moved in and in wasn't until the 1930's until they changed their names to Dewhurst. Back in 2016 when I took this picture Deerheart had just left for their new location at No.45, and in 2016 the building was the home of IHBA, which is an Industry Hair & Beauty Academy. Moving on to 2019 the shop has become the home of MJ training which specialises in first aid training.

No.207, London Road South.

In 1892 the shop was the home of Mr Craske who was a coal merchant, but by 1909 it had become a hairdressers owned by Charles Aldous. In 1922 it was recorded as still a hairdressers but now it's owned by Robert Keable, but by 1925 it had changed its use again to become a tobacconist run by William Stafford and then in the 1950's by Sidney Wilson. In the 1960's it became Reg Regis, I wasn't sure about this picture, but the roofs match and the address is correct if you line up the roof and signage with next door at No.209. Today in 2019 it is the home of Veriannes Dancewear.

No.209, London Road South.

 In 1909 the shop was the home of Frank Wheatly and his trade was a draper and in addition to this shop he had 211-213. In 1922 Frank had gone and the shop had become London Central Meats and then in the 1930's Freeman Harvey & Willis moved in and left their mark, literally. In the 1970's the shop along with next door was the home of Reg Regis and if you compare with the sign on the picture on page 49 you can see Shadow Sports & Embroidery reused Reg's sign.

 Before Shadow Sports, it was open for a short time as a chinese takeaway, it's been empty now for a good few years and time and neglect is starting to show on the window woodwork.

No.211-213, London Road South.

In 1892 No.211 or rather No.89 was a Drapers owned and run by H Jefferies who at the same time had a store in the High Street. By 1909 it had become one large shop with Frank R Wheatly having it as his drapers shop, but by 1925 the shop had passed to W. A. Robinson who too was a draper. By the time the late 30's came along Robinson changed his occupation, because the shop was then renamed; Robinson Cine & Photographic Service, Developing & Printing. The building was then called Manchester House. After the War the building became Boots but replaced in the 1960's by Saveway's- house furnishers, but by the 1970's it was Cavey's Discount Stores. In 2017 it was Spoked and now in 2019 Windsor Gallery moved in.

No.215, London Road South.

In 1892 No.215 was still a private house and the home of Mr. G. Brown. Mr Brown's occupation was that of a joiner and as well as that he was a bandmaster of the rifle volunteers.

By 1909 the building had been converted into a shop and was a grocers run by the partnership of Mr Murrills and Mr Miller. As well as operating from No.215, they also had No.217.

Listed in the 1922 copy of Kelly Directory Harry Muttett had taken over the shop and set up as a pork butchers and stayed open well into the late 1970's.

Since the butchers left, the shop has had many uses, but the most common use is that of a takeaway and in 2018 it is the home of the New Embassy Hong Kong.

It offers Exotic Cantonese and Peking Cuisine, so why not put down the book, pick up the phone and treat yourself to a takeaway today.

No.217, London Road South.

In 1892 the directory just says private house and in 1909 the building along with next door at No.215 is the grocers run by Murrills & Miller. By the 1920's the shop had switched from apples to fish and was a fishmongers owned and run by Sidney Thurston and he carried on running the business right up to the 1950's when the business then passed to his son, a Mr J. G. Thurston. By the 1970's the building was empty and in 2019 it is the home of Olympic Print. It says on their website; Olympic Print has been established over 20 years! We are a family business with lots of experience. We pride ourselves in delivering the highest quality work we can offer.

No.219-221, London Road South.

 In 1892 the building was split into two buildings and in No.92 which is now No.219 was Mr. J. King who was trading as baker & confectioner. Next door at No.93 which is now No.221 was Langley dairy supply and was run by R. B. Simons. By 1909 the building was knocked into one and became Stead & Simpsons and the only clue is the fading sign on the side of the building. Before Desmonds Ristorante Est 1990 moved in the shop was Marmaris Kebab & Pizza and still listed on the internet is Lowestoft Barbecue, still has opening times and phone number on 118118.

 Meanwhile on Desmonds facebook page it says; With more front than Lowestoft, the best pizza's for miles, tastiest shakes, home-made sponges, non-fried breakfast and the best coffee in town. Great guy, great place! Sadly this year in 2019 its back to an empty shop.

No.223, London road south.

In 1892 the house was the home of Mr. J. Baster, who's occupation was that of a shipwright, but by 1909 a Mr. Boddy set up shop as a bootmaker. From 1916 until the mid-20's a Mr Charles Metcalf had moved in and set up his photographic studio until in 1925 according to the Kelly Directory he had switched to be a radio dealer. By 1934 Metcalf had gone and the shop became Lowestoft Piano Store, selling pianos and musical instruments. At the end of the Second World War Mr Bedwell had gone and the shop became Speedy Repair Service, Boot & Shoe Repair and carried on late into the 1990's by Mr Normanston. Since then it's been Strand Electrical Store, Klash Photography and even a clown called andy for hire, now its Fancy Dress.

No.225-227, London Road South.

In 1892 No.225/No.96 was the home of Mr C Harper who was a cab driver, but by 1909 the shop was a pork butchers run funnily enough by a Mrs Butcher. By 1922 an Albert Freestone had opened the shop as a newsagents and he carried on well into the 1960's when the shop passed to Mr Hodgson who named it funnily enough Hodgson's Newsagents.

Moving on to No.227/No.97 was the home of Mr M Lambert who had already converted the building and was running it as fruiterer. In 1909 Mrs Hovells had set up shop as a dairy and it carried on in that role until the late 1960's. It changed ownership to Richard Stebbings in 1922 and then to Harry Balls in 1925 with finally passing to his son a Mr Samuel Balls in the late 1940's.

In the Kelly Directory of 1972 the dairy was gone, and the shop had become a fishmongers.

Today in 2019 both buildings are now combined, and the location of Kirkley Newsagents, the only newsagents on the whole of London Road South.

No.229, London Road South.

Established over 50 years.

MASCOT SHOES
FOR LADIES

Are the last word in inexpensive elegance and real comfort in LADIES' FOOTWEAR.

Shoes 8/11. Boots 12/9.

Mascot Shoes have a distinction possessed by no other Shoe offered at the price.

Best, Quickest and Cheapest Shop for Repairs.

FORD & Co.,

Family Boot Makers.

229, London Road South, LOWESTOFT.

In 1892 Ford & Co were operating from the address and carried on well into the 1930's before Barclays Bank set up business at the address.

Today in 2019 both No.229 & No.231 have combined and the address has been taken over by Rainbow Credit Union, when you compare the advert from circa 1900 to present day the upper building hasn't changed that much, even the drainpipes look the same.

No.231, London Road South.

 In 1892 it was the private home of Mr T Farrow who was an engine driver but by 1909 the shop was built, and a G. J. King had set up his tobacconist in the building. By the 1920's Herbert Cooper had taken over and set himself up as a newsagent and carried on up to the Second World War until Reg Regis sports outfitters moved in. Reg Regis carried on in the building until it moved into No.207-209 London Road South. At around that point of leaving Barclays took over the whole building.

Today in 2019 Rainbow Credit Union has the whole building.

No.233-239, London road South.

Firstly, if you can see on the right of the picture, you should see the original outline of the now removed terrace, which the new building has replaced. Back in 1892 No.233 was No.102 and was F. C. Payne who were greengrocers & provision merchants. In 1909 No.233 was Mackenzie & Ball, Needle Depot and No.235 was John Fisher Cabinet Makers, with No.237-239 being the Co-Operative.

By the 1920's the Lowestoft Co-operative Society Ltd had full control of the terrace of four buildings and the building we see today came into form.

Coming to think about it, The Co-Operative food is the only supermarket on London Road South.

No.241, London Road South.

 In this postcard on the right taken around 1909 you can clearly see the Co-Operative with its ornate gas lamps hanging out front of their shop and you can just make out the name Edwin Dorling, greengrocers just where the young boy is walking past. Frank Dorling was running the business from the 1920's and carried on well into the 1960's. In recent years the shop has been a few different businesses, second-hand shops and like you can see in the old picture from 2016 it was Pathways. In 2018 it was Symbols Barber Shop, today in 2019 it's another mini market.

No.243, London Road South.

In 1892 No.243 was listed in the directory as a private house, but by 1909 the shop was the home of Miss Forest who ran it as a stationer and post office. You can see on the previous page the post office and by 1922 a Mr Walter William Wiggett had taken over as postmaster. By the mid 1920's William Thomas Weeks had taken over the shop and was selling fancy goods. Within fifteen years the fancy goods were gone and replaced with radios as a Mr Holtom had set up shop as a wireless dealer. In 1972 the shop was J. M. Bird's cycle shop and along with bikes he sold the odd gun. In 2016 the shop was Lola Kitchen and today it's Millers chip shop.

No.245, London Road South.

 From day one this shop has always been a butchers, and in 1909 a Mr F Miller was running the shop. By 1922 the shop had passed to a Mr Horace Copeman who also traded as a butcher and he stayed well into the mid 1930's. In 1934 the shop was listed as belonging to William Firmin and he stayed right up to 1956 when the shop finally passed to Kenneth E Hutson.

 After Hutson's the shop stopped being a butchers and started its life passing from owner to owner, first it was Each, then in 2016 it was the K.A.S.A Project and in 2018 it was Brainwave. On their Facebook page it says; The purpose of the charity is to raise funds to support individuals with disabilities, that are less fortunate and have nobody to support or guide them.

No.249-257, London Road South.

In 1892 No.249 was the home of Mr H Garrould who traded as a shoemaker, but by 1909 No.249-251 was the home of J Brett & Sons, Complete House Furnishers & China Sales. By 1922 Sydney Whatley Jr had moved in and set up shop as a baker, but by 1934 he had taken a partner and that was H. J. Reddish. By the late 1930's they took the whole block up to No.257 and by the end of the War Whatley may of left the partnership but he was still living upstairs in the flats. The advert on the right is from the 1960's and you can see what Reddish's had to offer. By 1970 the restaurant had gone and at No.249-255 Arthur Hollis was running his grocers from the address. In 2019 No.249 is the home of Chick King and the rest is Each, raising money for East Anglia's Children's Hospices.

No.259, London Road South.

In 1892 there were two businesses on the plot, one being E Welham who traded as builders and W. H. Dutt who were carriage builders- farriers and general blacksmiths. By 1909 the private house of Mr Welham had become Mrs Welham lodging house as Her husband had passed away. In the 1920's the blacksmith was gone, and his premises had become W. Coleman & Co motor garage, but by the 1930's the garage had passed to Arthur McKenzie.

After the War the site became R. M. Wood coach builders & cellulose sprayers and their phone number was just 14. By the late 1960's the building we see today was being built and would become the East Anglian Trustee Saving Bank, but today the bank has made way for the Waveney Centre.

No.261-263, London Road South.

In 1892 the buildings were No.114-115 and both in the Shreeve family and the building was then called Eastbourne House. In 1909 the shop was owned by Mrs Kerrison who is just listed as shopkeeper, but by 1922 Reginald William Lockwood was in residence running his hairdressing business. In the 1930's the hairdressers had passed to Bertie Prigg and he carried on right into the 1980's. Since then No.261 has been a few different businesses namely A Piece of Café and in 2018 Raja Mahal.

Next door at No.263 since then it's has been Bruce S gents hairdressers then Bruce barbers and now in 2019 First computers.

No.265, London Road South.

In 1892 the area the now shop sits on was that of an empty plot, but in 1909 in the newly built building a Mr John Fenn had set up shop as a draper. Mr Fenn carried on for a good few years before in 1922 a Mr F. J. Parker is listed in the Kelly Directory operating as an optician,

In 1934 the opticians had gone and replaced by Mr F Chipperfield's wireless shop, but after the Second World War it was all change.

In 1948 Mr F. H. Waterman was operating from the shop as a watchmaker and carried on in the address right into the 1960's. In recent years it's been Dream Cakes and Aphrodite Nail and Beauty, but today in 2019 it is the home of Coffee and Vapes.

On Coffee and Vapes Facebook page it says; Vaping e-liquids, cds, starter kits, mods, coils tanks, offers, support, advice and essentials, plus delicious hot and cold drinks to drink in or takeaway.

No.267, London road South.

IF it's Flowers, Pot Plants, Fruit, Veg., Why not....

"CLARE'S"

★ PERSONAL ATTENTION ★

267 LONDON ROAD SOUTH
LOWESTOFT · SUFFOLK
TEL: 2263

In 1909 the shop was owned by A Brown who was just listed as a shop keeper, but by the 1920's Harry Roll had taken over the shop and opened as a greengrocers. Harry carried on through the Second World War and shortly after the business moved to A & M Knights and he also was a greengrocers. In the 1970's the shop was still a grocers but also sold flowers, pot plants and "Clare's" offered the personal touch. In recent years it's been Home Pc Fix and today in 2019 its Radiance hair salon.

No.269, London Road South.

In 1909 Walter George Fuller had the shop selling push bikes as in the Kelly Directory he was listed as a cycle agent. By 1920 the shop had passed to Philip George Wall who was trading as a picture frames maker, by the 1950's George looks like he had given up making picture frame and turned his hand to photography as the shop was now listed in the phonebook as photographers.

Only in recent years the shop has gone through a few owners but today in 2019 the present owner is Chriscott and I think I'm right in saying it the only independent domestic appliance dealer in town? But saying that who else can repair your washing machine?

No.271, London Road South.

In 1909 Albert H Moore owned the shop and was operating out of it as a fishmonger, but by the 1920's the shop had passed to Daniel Overy who also was a fishmonger.

At the end of the 1920's the shop had turned from selling fish to meat with William Tubby taking over but by the end of the Second World war it was all change again. Listed in 1948 the shop was listed as Forder's Drapers but by the 1952 directory it had turned into Mrs Brame Drapers. Listed in 1972 the shop was then Steller Greeting Cards and since then it's been East Coast kids, Bridal Parasol and now in 2019 Homewood & Rose, a home interiors paradise.

No.273, London Road South.

Once upon a time there was a terrace of three houses under this block of flats, but for its whole life No.273 was a private house.

In 1909 the house was occupied by a Mrs Johnson.

In 1922 the house was occupied by a Mrs Weaving.

In 1934 the house was then occupied by a Mrs C Stubbings.

In 1938 the resident was Mrs Sanham who stayed well into the 1970's and then it was flats.

No.275-277, London Road South.

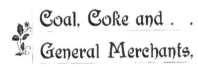

Coals! Coals! Coals!

THOMAS MOY, Limited,

Coal, Coke and . .
General Merchants,

Office—HARLEY HOUSE, LONDON ROAD,

TELEPHONE No. 33.   LOWESTOFT.

Branch Order Office—275, LONDON ROAD SOUTH.

Depots—G. E. Railway, Commercial Road, and Mid. & G. N. Joint, North Station.

Head Office—COLCHESTER; also Depots, Norwich, Ipswich, Great Yarmouth, Beccles, and throughout the Eastern Counties, and in London.

ALL ORDERS RECEIVE PROMPT & CAREFUL ATTENTION.

DELIVERED BY OUR OWN CARTS IN TOWN AND DISTRICT.

LEWIS T. JOHNSON, District Manager.

Quotations for Truck Loads to any G. E. Railway Station.

In 1909 No.275 was the home of Thomas Moy who traded as a Coal Merchant & Colliery Agent. By the 1920's William George Skinner had set up shop as a bootmaker but that was short lived as by 1925 Herbert N Gaze was operating as a pork butcher.

In 1909 Thomas Moy was using No.277 as well as next door but by 1920 the shop changed ownership to a Mrs F. N. Brown. She lived there right up to the end of this building but sometime in the 1950's she set up shop as a confectioner at the address.

Today as you can see from the picture on page 70 the block of three has been replaced by flats.

No.285-287, London Road South.

With No.285 it wasn't until the 1920's that the house was converted to a shop, up to that point it was the home of a one Mr Price Hamer. In the 1920's a Mr Watkins & Son set up shop as ladies & gentlemen hairdressers. They stayed put right up to the late 1970's.

Moving on to No.287 in 1909 it was home to the Haily family with a Charles Haily listed at the address and it wasn't until the late 1930's until it was converted to a shop. In 1938 the shop was the premises of W. J. Fletcher, pork butcher, but it the mid 50's it was taken over by Hodgson's who carried on until the 1980's. For many years these shops laid empty and an eyesore and it wasn't until recently they were converted back in private residence.

No.289-291, London Road South.

No.289 in 1909 was the private home of Mrs E Beale, but by the 1920's she had moved on and a Mr George Albrow took residence. In 1938 Ernest Hutson jr moved in and it wasn't until the 1950's that the house was converted into a shop with frontage.

In 1952 the shop was listed in Kelly Directory as a greengrocers being run by a Mrs E. B. Duckerin. In the 1972 phone book the building had passed to C & S Electrical Ltd run by a Mr K. Mullard. The shop specialised in radio & televisions etc.

Next door at No.291 was a different story as it stayed as a private house until the 1970's until a business moved in and that was Ansdell Taxis. I must say from what I can remember about the shops they looked better back as flats.

No.297, London Road South.

In my lifetime I can say I've never seen this shop ever open, but nevertheless it was Arthur Peck's Boot & Shoe Dealer and Repairer & Chiropodists since the 1930's. Up to that point it was the home in 1909 to a Mr John Daniel Hamer and in 1924 it was the home of an Arthur William Wood. This building looks the same as what No.285-287-289 and 291 would of looked like if they were not converted back. If you look carefully you can see where the bay window has been removed on the first floor to allow the ground floor to be extended. I think if the shop is not reopened it awaits the same fate, either a house or flats?

No.299, London Road South.

No.299 hasn't changed in anyway really since it was built and in 1909 it was the private home of Mrs Johnson.

In the 1925 Kelly Directory a Mr Henry William Anderson had moved in and it wasn't until 1930 that he was replaced by a William Curson Jr.

After the Second World War a lady called Suzanne moved in and set up shop from her front room as Suzanne's ladies hairdressers, but by 1972 it was Miss Janet's Ladies hairdressers.

The building has laid empty for some while but is just a private home today.

No.301, London Road South.

In 1909 the house was the private house of a Mr Henry Howell Vincent and listed in the phone book in 1925 he was replaced with a Mr John Asher Barker.

By the 1930's it was still a private house and like next door a lady called Kathleen had set up shop from her front room cutting ladies hair. Come 1938 a G. C. Mantripp had moved in and carried on cutting ladies hair like the previous owner.

Come the end of the Second World War the shop had been converted and had become Albert Manning's Confectioners with him carrying on until the 1970's when Frank Ball moved in from next door when he needed more space. Frank Ball as well as having No.301 also had 303.

In 2018 the shop was the home of Lowestoft Watersports and specialised in kiteboarding, kitesurfing, stand-up paddle-boarding, wake-boarding, surfing, kayaking and canoes. Today in 2019 the shop has closed down and is awaiting a new tenant.

No.303, London road South.

In 1909 the building was still a private house and in the hands of Mrs M Marsden but by 1925 ownership had moved to a Mr John Albert Evans.

After the Second World War Frank Ball moved in and Set about converting it into his newsagents but by the 1970's he needed more room, so he took over No.301.

In recent years it was Kitchen Delights and lastly until this year 303 Eaterie, British-Vegetarian friendly & Vegan options.

On trip advisor it has 4.5 stars out of 5 and the last review left on the 1st July 2018 reads as follows; We recently had a lovely stay at 303 Eaterie. Caroline & Charlie are most hospitable, warm & Friendly. Lovely-food, would highly recommend this B & B & bistro.

As you can see the shop is now closed down so another shop on London Road South has an unknown future?

No.305, London Road South.

In 1909 this was Dagmar House and it was owned by a Mrs Fairchild who ran it as a boarding house. By 1925 the boarding house had passed to a Wilfred Cook and at the same time he owned the Towers at No.311.

Around the 1930's the building when under a facelift and became the home of Lloyds Bank in London Rd South. Listed in the phone book in 1952 a Clifford Howard but as the years rolled on and long before the banking world started closing branches because they say we are doing in more online it closed. It was one of the last big banks to go from the road and now in 2019 no bank exists south side of the bridge apart from the odd cash machine.

No.307, London Road South.

Today No.307 or Stanley House is in a right royal mess but in 1909 it was the home of H. C. Buckler who ran the shop as a grocer.

By 1922 the grocers passed to a Mr Arthur Blackwell who traded as Blackwell's Grocers and Provisions, but by 1925 it just has a Mrs Blackwell listed at the address so not sure if Mr Blackwell had passed away?

The building carried on as Blackwells right up to the end of the 1970's but in recent years it was Mr Wendals extreme lifestyle shop.

If you can find its web page it states; Mr Wendals is an extreme lifestyle shop for all you skateboard, motocross, bmx, scooter fans, we will be selling all the t shirts, hoodys, elbow and knee protection, helmets, kits, parts and accessories. Plus, to keep you refreshed in the summer we will be introducing a Hawaiian ice cream machine as well as red bull and monster energy drinks.

Sadly, like everything today the internet has had a big impact on the high street and everything on that long list can be easily picked up online with free postage. The general populations shopping habits have just changed, with one click you can buy something online and have it delivered by the next day rather than going out and supporting these shops which have all gone and are going to the wall.

No.309, London Road South.

 In 1909 W. L. Sanders was operating as a chemist along with Cross & Co selling china and glass from the same address. By the 1920's Cross & Co was gone and along with the chemist A. Crisp & Son had joined them selling stationary. Mr Sanders carried on at the address until the 1960's when the business passed to a R. V. Fisher but by then Sanders had added an opticians to the business. In recent years the Co-Operative pharmacy was operating from the building but since they left it's just been sitting empty waiting for its next lease of life. If you compare the postcard from 1909 you can see since the picture was taken the bay window has gone and also a chimney where the present-day boiler vent pipes are coming out of the external wall.

Lowestoft Methodist Church.

The picture on the left is taken from the Hook family archive and shows the land before the church was built. The land on the left is the grounds of the former St. Aubyn's College, which was a public school, the remains of which can still be seen today if you look for them. The tower next door acted as their boarding house and the garage behind used to act as their classrooms. The picture clearly pre-dates the introduction of the trams and what a crowd watching the parade.

No.637, London Road South.

It wasn't until the 1930's that the house was converted into a shop and in 1934 Ada Bartle & Rhoda Holt opened their confectioners.

The pair carried on until the late 1940's when the building became Mr H Wrights Café, but by the 1950's the café was gone and replaced by H Wright- Grocer & Post Office.

In 1972 P. E. Allerton took over as postmaster and the grocers had gone only to be replaced with a toy shop. It carried on for years and it wasn't until recent years it was converted into two shops.

In 2018 You have Knight Vision Opticians & Eyewear, and on the right, you have Little Bird, it says simply on Facebook. Card & Gift shop located in Pakefield. Moving on in 2019 little bird has gone and Knights Vision has the whole building.

No.639, London Road South.

This is the last number on the street and marks the end of the odd numbers. In 1934 Owen Gray opened his hairdressers at No.639 and combined it with a post office.

In 1938 Owen Gray was still there but the hairdressers had gone, but no sooner than the Second World War was over a T. C. Cook had taken over as a grocer as well as running the post office. By 1950 the post office had moved next door and the building was once occupied by Owen Grey who appears has put down the scissors and replaced them with a hammer and re-opened as a builders and iron mongers. By the 1970's the shop had become Terminus Stores, a fruit and veg shop, today in 2019 the shop is no longer Irene's House of Flowers, but Flora & Fern Flowers.

No.136, London Road South.

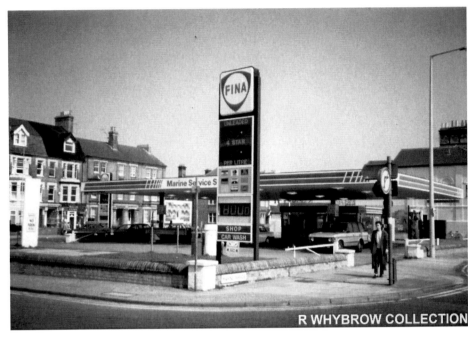

 Up to the 1950's all this area was surrounded by a six-foot high wall, lined with trees and was the private estate of a doctor. In 1957 the house and grounds were sold, and the bull dozers moved in on the estate with the only little sections of wall left in place to remember it was once there.

 In 1957 work commenced on building Marine Parade Filling Station and in the picture on the left from the Robert Whybrow collection you can see the garage was a Fina station and I can tell you back then it was roughly £1.65 a gallon. In 2006 KFC upped sticks from Station Square and moved onto the site but unlike the petrol station they didn't keep the London Road South address and number but today they are listed at Marine Parade.

No.138, London Road South.

In the 1920's No.138 was the home of the Lowestoft Co-Operative Society Butchers, but before that there was no listings for the address. After the butchers the shop next appears in the phone book in 1972 as Austins, fried fish shop and then started this shops association with fast food and takeaway.

Today in 2019 the shop is Kings kebab house and prior to that was Seven Stars Takeaway, you can see on the picture on the right evidence that the co-op was once there. I suppose we are lucky it hasn't been chipped of and removed.

No.140-142, London Road South.

today in 2019 Fashion Clean appears to take up both buildings.

It's a bit of an industrial looking building, plain and boring, featureless but today in 2019 it is Fashion clean. It's rare in this town being a dry cleaners as I think it's one of the only ones within the town, southside at least.

In 1972 No.140 was the home of Christine, ladies hairdressers and next door at No.142 was Studio Three selling everything you need to be an artist.

In the 1980s No140 was the home of a ladies hairdressers called BJs.

In more recent years No.140 was Waveney Locksmiths but

No.144, London Road South.

No.144 has laid empty now for the last few years and in its life has been a few different things.

In 1972 the building was John Blundell house furnishers. I remember as a kid being dragged in there to look round the stalls when it was turned into a market shop.

In 2006 Hovells opened a store in the building and it carried on up to August 2012 when the rise on online shopping caused the downfall of this giant. Hovells were operating online but they blamed the comparison website which would allow shoppers to find the items cheaper.

No.146, London Road South.

In 1972 the hotel before it was a hotel was the home of H. M. Inspector of taxes, but after the taxman left it became the Royal Court Hotel.

The Hotel was being used as a temporary shelter for homeless people in the town, but after complaints about the state of the hotel the local council forced it to close.

Since it closed some ten years ago it has slowly been rotting but nevertheless the hotel has found a new owner and is awaiting a new lease of life.

No.148-152-154, London Road North.

SOUTH LOWESTOFT
SEA WATER
SWIMMING BATHS
(FINEST IN ENGLAND)

OPEN ALL DAY.   ADMISSION 6d. EACH.

HAPPY TIMES AT THE BATHS.

Family Bathing : Sundays 7 a.m. to 9 a.m. Weekdays 7 am. to 9 p.m.

Swimming Lessons by Swimming Expert. 2/6 per Lesson. 12 Lessons £1 1s.

SEA WATER PRIVATE BATHS
(HOT OR COLD).

Invaluable to those suffering from Rheumatism.

Visitors run down in health are invited to try these as a "Pick-me-up."
Medical Men recommend them.

WEEKDAYS, 7 A.M. TO 9 P.M.   SUNDAYS, 7 A.M. TO 9 A.M.
1/6 each, or Book of 12 Tickets 15/-.

A. G. CUTTS, Lessee and Manager.

R WHYBROW COLLECTION

In 1909 the site was listed as South Lowestoft Swimming & Private Baths, run by one Alfred Cutts. By the 1930's the pool had been filled in and the pipes running for the sea were closed off and the cinema had taken over. The Grand cinema carried on well up to the 1970's when it changed use again and this time into the Grand Sporting Club. Since the building was rebuilt it has been the Kirkley Centre. There is also a listing in 1972 for No.154 for the Mclary coin operated laundry who were operating for the address.

No.156a-156b, London Road South.

 In 1892 J Utting Yallop was operating out of the building running his cabinet and picture framing business and at No.156b George Durrant was operating his fruitier and green grocers business from the address before he was to move to No.161. In the picture on the left you can see the extension to 156 over the building on the right and 156b would of extended under the bay window. In 1909 Mr Yallop was still in the building but now he was listed as a print seller, but by the 1930's John Devereux & Sons who already operated from No.156 simply took the rest over and set up as high-class tobacconists. In 1972 A. W. Cooke moved in as a tobacconist and ten years later replaced by London Colney Coaches, but since then it's been Intergifts, Beckham Photography and now in 2019 I do Venue Styling.

No.156, London Road South.

In 1892 John Devereux & Sons were operating from the address as grocers & provision merchants and carried on in the address until the 1970's when a M. S. Tripp took over as a fruitier.

In the picture on the right the building had become Gamares fully licenced restaurant but for all the time I can remember it, it has been Red Rose Florist. Looking at the building it really hasn't changed that much architecturally speaking it has just had a sand blast down to its original brick colour, oh and there's a tree in front of it.

No.158, London Road South.

In 1892 the building was the premises of a W. Barber who was operating from the address as bootmakers, but by 1909 he was gone, and it had been taken over by Harold E Bird who set up shop as jewellers. By the 1920's Mr Bird was gone, and his jewellers had been replaced by another boot makers and this it was Austin Shoe Co. We shouldn't forget between the late 1890's and 1909 in was the offices of the Lowestoft Women's Suffrage Society, I like the comment on the window banner about them being non-militant. By 1925 John Durrant had moved in and was operating as a fruiterer from the address, by the 1930's George took over and stayed until the 1950's when it turned from fruit to hair. In the 1952 phone book an Ernest Weavers had opened his hairdressers from No.158, by the 1970's the shop had become Roy's snack bar. In 1980 the building was the home of Prontoprint up to the point Hunny Bee Vintage moved in. On their Facebook page it says; Vintage & Retro curios & collectables for sale, gifts and handmade crafts. Sit & relax, enjoy a taste of a bygone era with a delicious cream tea.

No.160, London Road South.

In 1892 Mr T Lathbridge, pork butcher was operating from the address. By 1909 the International Tea Company Stores Ltd had moved in and carried on operating until the 1930's. In 1934 a Mr Sydney Albert Watkins set up business as a ladies hairdressers, it was very short lived as by 1938 Mrs Burwood had opened her Confectioners. In 1950 a Mrs Vera Porter opened up as a café, but this is where it gets weird as in 1957 the phone book has a William Burwood Jn running his café but by 1972 Vera Porter was back. She carried on into the 1990's, during the 1980's Vera reopened as a I'L Bistro, 3 course lunch on Sunday & a La Carte lunches every day and within twenty years at the age of 87 in 2000 she died.

In the picture above from the Robert Whybrow collection you can see in the 1990's the shop was General Custer and since then it spent a time as Speedy Peppers and today in 2019 it is the home of Pizza Time.

No.162, London Road South.

In 1892 No.162 was the home of Mr E Payne who traded as a butchers, but by 1909 the butchers shop had passed to Benjamin Sanders who also at the same time had another store at No.133 in the High Street. In the Kelly Directory in 1925 the butchers shop had changed hands again and this time into the hands of Frederick W Rackham, but again in the Kelly's book it changed hands again to William Jaques Fletcher who guess again was another butcher. During the Second World War the Hannant's shop in London Road North was heavily damaged and was forced to relocate but decided to keep the store open Southside as well as the new one at No.56 London Rd North. During the 1970's the shop carried on as Betty's wool shop and in the 1980's it was Heidi's. In 2018 The Green Lady Eco Store is in residence, it says on Facebook that the store is the place for hand-picked eco-friendly, ethical, organic & vegan products for your everyday needs. But today in 2019 the shop is being renovated into a shop called Way Up High which will specialise in selling preloved children's items.

No.164, London Road South.

In 1892 the shop was Frederic Masterson operating as a tailor & draper and carried on until the 1940's. Around the mid 40's the shop became Collins & Smith, radio dealer and carried on as an electronic shop. In 2018 East Coast Hospice charity shop had the building.

No.166, London Road South.

In 1892 the shop was under the ownership of Mr. F. W. Sparham & was running it as the Convent Garden Shop, but by 1909 Edward Soons who already had a store in the High Street had a second shop at this location. By the time the 1930 phone book was out the store had passed to Mrs Anna Nunn, who too was a greengrocer, but in the 1940's the shop had passed to Dann & Son who were tackle dealers. In the 1972 Kelly's Directory the shop was listed as Lowestoft Engraving, but in 2019 the shop is no longer empty and now is Lowestoft Ink.

No.168, London Road South.

In 1892 the shop was the home of Mr Walter James Norris who was trading as a watchmakers. He carried on until the 1940's when ownership passed to Fenton's Fashions, Mr P Fenton proprietor trading as a gown shop. In the 1952 phonebook the shop had then passed to Reliance Photographic Services but before 1957 it had then become Kwick Cleaners who funnily enough were dry-cleaners. In the shops last incarnation, it was Lockdales and was a main dealer for metal detectors and brought and sold coins and I suppose anything the detectorist dug up? Today in 2019 it's for sale, so if you have £160,000 it could be yours?

No.170-172, London Road South.

Starting at No.170 it was the home in 1909 to Searles & Wilton who were plumbers and stayed at the address until the late 1930's. In 1934 the shop was the home to Madame Betty who traded as a ladies hairdressers. By the late 1940's the shop had become Scotch Café under the ownership of a Mr. E. J. Crichton, but by the 1970's it had turned to Butler menswear and today it's one half of Armstrong & North opticians.

No.172 in 1909 was Samuel Webster Turner's confectioners shop, but by the end of the War it had past to Porter & Andrew who traded as electrical contractors. By the 1950's the shop had passed to E. H. Andrews, who were motorcycle dealers. Now it's the second half of Armstrong & North.

No.174-176, London Road South.

 In 1909 the building started its long association with being a fish and chip shop with Harold Cladingbowl who in 1922 passed the business on to Albert Drewitt who had it as his fried fish shop. By 1934 the shop had been taken over by William barker but not for long as by 1938 a Thomas Cook had taken over the chip shop. After the Second World War the shop was taken over by a Mr Harry Gallagher who had it as his fish restaurant but by the 1950's it had become Micky's Carlton Fish Restaurant and in the 1970's Micky knocked through into next door to make the shop the way we see it today. Today in 2018 the chip shop is the Trawlerman, offering traditional fish and chips and restaurant or take away. No.176 in 1909 was the home of Gwyn William who ran the shop as a stationers, but by the 1920's the shop became Currys Ltd who started off as cycle dealers in London Rd South. In the 1950's they quit the road and carried on trading at No.59 London Rd North. In the 1950's the shop was taken over by Home Hobbies and then in 1970 Micky knocked through from next door.

No.178-180, London Road South.

No.178 in 1909 a Bert Cullingford was trading out of the shop as a pork butcher, but shortly after the Bombardment of Lowestoft Edgar & Co moved into the building after their shop was destroyed. He stayed well into the 1950's when the shop passed to a Mr S Chilvers who sold house furnishings. Recorded in the 1972 phone book it had Cook's Furnishings at the address. In recent years the shop was more known for being Morlings but today it is Paul Hubbard.

No.180 in 1892 E. J. P. Fisher operated from the address as a hairdresser but in 1909 it was the home of Miss Maria Leech confectioners shop, it stayed at the address until the late 1930's when it became Mr Douglas Reed's fruiterers. After the Second World War Reed was gone and replaced by the Covent Garden fruiterers and then by 1972 it passed to N & B Whiting another fruitier. Not long after that Morlings moved in but like their shop in London Road North it closed and the London Road South one followed at about the same time. Today like next door is now Paul Hubbard sales & lettings.

No.182, London Road South.

Directors: GEO. H. TAYLOR, F.C.I.A.
W. E. DURRANT, M.R.San.I.

PALMERS

(GEOFFREY E. PALMER & CO. LTD.)

HOUSE AND ESTATE
AGENTS, VALUERS
AND
INSURANCE BROKERS

★ ★ ★

182 LONDON ROAD SOUTH
LOWESTOFT

Established 1919

Telephone : Lowestoft 128
(After Hours 839 or 1725)

LOCAL OFFICE :
LEEDS PERMANENT BUILDING SOCIETY

See Street Plan E6

In 1892 the building was called Leadenhall House and the private home of Miss Moore, but by 1909 it was Archibald Westley Mobbs butchers. By 1922 the shop had passed to Ernest John Hutson who ran it as a dairy and carried on trading until the 1940's when the shop passed then to a Mr R Mallett who carried on the business as a dairy.

As you can see from the advert on the right the next to own the building was Palmers house and estate agents, valuers and insurance brokers. In the 1972 edition of the Kelly Directory the business had passed to Peter E Soper and Partners who were also estate agents.

Today in 2019 the shop belongs to William Hill and is the only bookies on London Road South, my nanny loves the horses and at 86 she likes nothing more than putting on her 20p each way bet!

No.184, London Road South.

 To be honest this shops signage has upset me as you can clearly see the old signage has been removed rather than being covered over, just hope it hasn't been skipped? From the 1900's until the 1960's it was the home of The Home and Colonial Ltd. Since then it has been many different types of stores including takeaways the latest being one called Good View Takeaway. Today in 2019 the shop has become London Minimarket.

No.186, London Road South.

In 1892 the building was the home of Mr Charles. B. Buxton who traded out of the shop as a saddler. In 1909 Charles was still operating but not for long because in 1922 the saddle-makers was gone, and a Mr Charles Edwin Field had reopened the shop as his restaurant.

In the Kelly Directory for 1934, World Stores Ltd a provision shop was open at the address and carried on trading well into the late 1960's.

In the 1972 Kelly Directory Dorlings fruiterers had set up business, but since then it's been through a lot of different owner with the last being Suffolk House Florists.

Today in 2019 the shop is now Gifted Emporium. On Facebook it simply says; Gifted emporium supplies fabrics, haberdashery, handmade gifts, up-cycled, craft needs, upholstery.

No.190, London Road South.

In 1892 No.190 or as it was Wellington House was the home of Durrant & Son who were fruiterers. This family seem to shift up and down this street between the years getting a bigger shop every time, but nevertheless in 1909 they we still he but listed as a florist.

By 1925 Durrant & Son was gone again and Walpoles moved in and set up shop as a confectioners, but by 1938 the confectioner business had passed to Mrs E Leighton who carried on for another 8 years.

After the Second World War Prudential Assurance moved in and started trading selling their policies but by the mid 1950's Prudential were gone to different premises on the road.

In the Kelly Directory for 1957 S. G. Matthams moved in and started his watchmakers business and by the 1980's he was still there.

In recent years the shop has been Bondi Beach Tan and Empire Hair Artistry but today in 2019 it is the home of Millie Rose Hair & Beauty.

No.194, London Road South.

In 1892 the building was called Oxford House and was the retail premises belonging to F. A. Cornish who was operating as a draper. By 1909 his wife E. A. Cornish was running the business, so not sure if he had passed? In the Kelly Directory of 1922 Miss Mildred Fraser was recorded running her milliner business from the shop, so now you know where everyone purchased their hats from on the road. In 1925 Benjamin Rogers moved in and set up his tailoring business and stayed trading at the address until the 1960's. By 1972 the business had passed to William Pickard and by the 80's it then became the home of Leather Luxe which was part of Walker-Regis. Today in 2019 it's a charity shop.

No.198-202, London Road South.

No.198-206 today is the home of Cooks, but before that they were all individual shops. No.198 in 1892 was the home of Kirkley Drug Stores run by a F. D. Jeacock and he stayed at the address until the 1930's when the chemist passed to Arthur Larder. After the War the shop became S & D Payne Restaurant, but by the 1950's it had become a grocers run by the Purdy family. In the 1960's Lilians who were next door knocked through.

No.200 or London House started out as Mr Freeman's Drapers but by 1909 he was gone, and the shop had passed to a Mr Dagley & Son who too were drapers. By the time the Kelly Directory was published in 1938 the shop had passed to Alfred Bunguard who carried on until the end of the 1940's as a draper when at that time the shop was taken over by Miss Lilian Spink who traded as drapers & ladies & childrens outfitters. Looking at the building you may also notice the upper floor of No.200-202 is missing, not sure what happened here? In the 1960's Chadds took over the business but it carried on trading under the Lilian's name until it closed in 1990 and Cooks took over the buildings, but sadly due to retirement the building all stands empty.

No.204-206, London Road South.

In 1892 No.204 was known as Hereford House and the business premises of Mr R Mays & Co who traded as boot makers. By 1909 Robert Mayes had taken over the boot making business and stayed until the 1930's when the building became H. H. Chaplin house furnishings. In the 1934 Kelly Directory a Mr H Roll had taken over the building and opened a fruit shop, and by 1952 the fruit shop had passed to A & M Knights. By 1970 the building had been expanded into by Lilians.

No.206 in 1892 was the home of Kirkley Café run by a Mr B Brown but by 1909 the shop had become a drapers run by a Mr J Fenn. By 1922 Ernest Hollowell had taken over the shop right up to the 1940's when a Kenneth Goff & Son who opened as a confectioner. Kenneth stayed right up to the 1970's when again Lilians took over the building and knocked through.

No.208, London Road South.

In 1892 No.208 was the home of R. May & Co who were bootmakers, but by 1909 May was gone and replaced by a outfitters run by Frank Albert Leighton. The business carried on right up to the mid 1920's and by that time Frank had knocked through to No.210. In the Kelly Directory in 1925 the shop was then owned by Mortimer Brundle who too was an outfitters, but by 1934 the shop was a florists under the ownership of Fokerd & Manthorpe, it was called Florette. In the 1940's it was a Boot & Shoe repair shop run by E. Mountney, but by 1952 it was a china dealers run by A. Beamish. By the 1970's it was a Turf Accountants run by G. Bailey. As a kid I do remember asking my dad what one was, and he told me it was a shop that sold turf. Since then it's been a few different shops but today in 2019 it's a beauticians.

No.210, London Road South.

In the year 1892 the shop belonged to Mr G Miller who traded as an upholster but by 1909 the shop became the home of Frank Leighton when he knocked though from next door.

By the 1930's the shop had passed to Mr F Stannard who traded as a gents outfitters but by the late 1930's Stannard was gone and replaced by N. J. Brundle who was also an outfitters.

At the end of the Second World War the new owner of the shop was a Mr E Mountney who was operating as a boot and shoe repair shop and the shop was still knocked through from next door so was operating in both No.208-210.

In the 1950's the shop was separated again and this time the shop was Markus Hosiery Co, dealing in hosiery and hosiery repair.

Taking over from Mr Markus was Took the bakers, who would eventually be taken over by Bushells.

No.212, London Road South.

The Plough & Sail, previously knowns as the Plough is located at No.212. The landlord in 1860 was Alfred Borrett and back then from his stables he used to rent horses and carriages.

Today in 2018 the stables are long gone as the motor car replaced the horse and carriage, but it has a good big of frontage if you want to sit out and have a drink.

On Facebook it has a good number of good reviews.

"Simply by far the best pub in Lowestoft. Best landlord & landlady. Best music, great staff and the greatest memories are made there!"

No.214 London Road South.

This building you would just write off as a garage, but I was surprised to work out it in fact has a number of 214. In 1892 this building was the home of Mr J Wood's corn and flour merchants, but by 1909 Parker & Godfrey had taken over as miller & merchants. By 1922 Mr Samuel Patterson took over the corn business and stayed well into the 1950's when a Mr Arthur Hollis took over. By the 1970's the building became Lowestoft Freezer Centre, but since then the door has gone and replaced with a window covered over with the plough and sail swing board attached to it. I remember it a while ago having a display in its window for the chemist which once was next door at No.216.

No.216, London Road South.

Up to the point it became Tinkerbelle this shop had always been a chemists. In 1892 the shop was run by a Mr G. E. Clarke who was a chemist & druggist but by 1909 the shop had passed to Coleman and Brown who stayed put until the 1980's. Since then it's been a number of different chemists, Kirkley Pharmacy, Eastpoint Pharmacy, Day Lewis pharmacy and Ingram Pharmacy.

Today in 2019 the building is Tinkerbelle Bridal Wear, and on their website, which is worth a good look it says; "Tinkerbelle was born in January 1989 when Pauline & husband Robert (with two young children) decided to open a shop in Lowestoft which specialized in beautiful bridal wear. If you look carefully you can just see my hairdresser's, Crosby's.

No.218-220, London Road South.

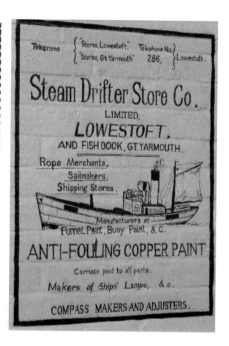

The Drifter started out its life as the Lord Raglan and during the 1860's the locals referred to it as Davey's bar after the landlords nick name, a great corner street pub a little smaller now than in previous years as it used to take up the terrace house next door along Claremont rd. I always remember the terraced house before it was converted to be full of pigeons.

The advert above is from 1983 and it says Tony and Su would like to extend a warm welcome to all customers old and new, a comment which is repeated in a review on the pubs Facebook page. "It's a lovely pub which treats all customers with respect and treats the regulars like family.

No.222-224, London Road South.

No.222 in 1892 was the home of John Sayers who was a tinplate worker & fancy dealer. By 1922 John had given up being a fancy dealer and opened the shop simply as an ironmongers.

In 1934 Mr & Mrs Starling opened the shop as a confectioners and tobacconists as well as selling wool, needlepoint, silks and fancy goods.

By the 1950's the shop had become Samuel Harris's greengrocers, but by the 1960's the building was absorbed into the Hailey's empire.

No.224 in 1892 was Brixton House and was Frederick Hailey plumbers & Tobacconist, by 1909 the plumbers part was gone, and it was just a tobacconist.

In the 1930's the Hailey's empire was growing and now had expanded into 226-228 & 230 and was called Hailey House furnishers.

Today in 2019 the original building is long gone and sits under the new Hailey House.

No.226-228-230, London Road South.

The Hailey's store was somewhat of a flagship store and sold just about everything under one roof. In an advert from 1922 it said; Hailey's-everything for the home, carpets, lino's, bedding, bedsteads, soft furnishings, wallpaper, china and glass etc. On the early morning of Saturday 22nd March 1980, a small fire broke out, but even though the fire was put out quickly too much stock was smoke damaged and the store never re-opened. I've got a friend who was telling me that the week before his future mother in law gave him and his future wife the money for some furniture for their new house and was worried it had been damaged in the fire, but luck would have it, it was moved to the Hailey's storage building and was safe. The building must of looked grand in its day with those blinds extended, such a shame it was pulled down, it must have been like working for Grace Brothers if you're old enough to get the reference.

No.232, London Road South.

This building is one of the rare ones, in that it stayed in the same ownership for 70 years and carried on doing the same thing for all those years. In 1892 it was owned by William Adamson and he traded for all that time until the 1960's as a grocers and dairy and in the pictures above you can see as the new owner cleaned off the paint the lovely green glazed tiles under the windows.

From the time Adamson left the shop it then spent a while as Laurie's Antique shop and had a few difference incarnations after that, its last was that of Beanie Mad for It, a gift shop, special occasion gifts and Novelty but mainly those stuffed bears everyone was going nuts for during the 2000's my mother included.

The new shop is Ivy Dreams its selling homewares and home interior items. Wish them the best of luck on their new venture.

No.234, London Road South.

 The building spent most of its early life as a private house with a Lionel W Collins living there in 1909 and then a Walter Ernest Cooper in 1922, but as with many other conversions on the road some of the architectural features have been removed, namely the upper bay windows.

 Recorded in the phone book of 1972 the building first appears as a shop and that shop is owned by Jo Ann fashions and I guess that was a ladies clothing shop. In my life-time I've only known this shop as Suffolk Aerial Installations and I spent a good bit of time it's there over the years buying electronic parts for my pinball machine collection. I think the new owners of this building did a wonderful job at converting this shop back to a house, it's a must see if you care to walk up London Road South and then you can pop in next door and buy something?

No.252, London Road South.

No.252 is another building which was converted from its original use as a private house, recorded in 1909 it was the home of a Mr R. D. Meller, but its 1925 when it first appears as a shop. In 1925 the shop belonged to a Robert Carter who was set up as a fine art dealer but recorded in the Kelly Directory for 1934 George Parr has arrived and the shop was still operating as a fine art shop/dealer as well as picture framers. In the 1950's the shop is recorded in the phone book as now being a book shop, but by 1957 the shop appears to have changed hands to an E & D Pease and still under the name of Parrs are operating as book sellers. From the advert above which is from the late 1960's you can see Parrs had then developed into the shop we know and love. I have so many great memories of this shop as a kid with my late grandad taking me in there to buy bits for my 00 trainset, it was and still is the best place in town to find model railway as Hannant's when it was open never had the same range or back catalogue Parrs has. I'm only 46 now so I'm planning to get another train set started when I hit 50.

No.264, London Road South.

In 1909 Misses A & A Graveling were operating the business as a confectioner, but by 1922 a Mrs Hannah Tench had taken over the business and was carrying on the confectionery business. In 1925 the business passed to V. H. Wood who too was, a confectioner who used to sell there-own, handmade cakes. After the confectioners the shop became J. J. Domestics selling appliances and repairing them, today in 2019 the shop is Chapz barber shop. On Facebook it says; "We are a barbers located in Kirkley. Hayley & Gill have worked locally for the last ten years and are a mother & daughter partnership."

Kington* House

A GUEST HOUSE OF DISTINCTION
ONE MINUTE FROM THE BEACH

¶ Comfortable Lounge.

¶ Separate tables in dining room.

¶ Bedrooms : Hot and cold running water, Interior spring mattresses throughout, gas or electric fires, bedside lights.

¶ 2 minutes from Claremont Pier, putting greens and promenade. Near Kensington Gardens and bowling greens. Close to buses for shops, theatres and cinemas.

¶ Good and liberal food.

¶ **Personal supervision by proprietors.**

MR. and MRS. C. JERMAIN
302 LONDON ROAD SOUTH

Terms : Board Residence 5-6 gns.   *Lowestoft 1467*

"EVINGTON" GUEST HOUSE✶

332 London Road South, Lowestoft.   Phone : Lowestoft 1314
Comfortable and homely Board Residence. One minute Sea and Kensington Gardens. Two minutes Claremont Pier and Shops. Well recommended. H. and C. all Bedrooms. Good Food. Personal attention. Separate Tables. Lounge and Garage. Open All the Year. Terms—Full Board, 4 to 5½ Gns., according to Season. B. & B. No restrictions.   (Late Coventry). Proprietors : **Mr. & Mrs. A. Twamley and Mrs. V. M. Carpenter**
See Street Plan E/6

MARGUERITE GUEST HOUSE

312 LONDON ROAD SOUTH, LOWESTOFT.   Phone Lowestoft 1025
Open all the year round. Ideally situated. One min. from sea, 2 mins. Claremont Pier and shops. H. & C. all bedrooms. Interior spring beds. "**All the Best**" for a really happy holiday. Very highly recommended. Terms, Full Board, Oct. to May 4 gns., May 4½ gns. June 5 gns., July and August 5½ gns., Sept., 5 gns.,   B. & B. *Proprietors :* **Mr. and Mrs. FRED J. GLOVER.**   See Street Plan E6

ELMA GUEST HOUSE

298 London Road South

Comfortable Board Residence   .   Excellent Food

Children Welcome   .   Conveniently Situated

Near Sea, Shops and Buses   .   Moderate Terms

Write for Tariff

Proprietress: Mrs. G. Robertson

Highly Recommended

See Street Plan E6

REALLY CHEERFUL HOMELY BOARD RESIDENCE

3 mins. Sea. Early Morning Tea and Four Good Meals. Baths. Children minded evenings. Interior Sprung Beds. All inclusive. No extras. From 3½ Gns. to 5 Gns., according to season.

Phone 586.   **COBLEY, 396 LONDON ROAD SOUTH.**
See Street Plan E/6

No.486-488, London Road South.

In 1925 the terrace only ran to No.482, but shortly after that No.486 became Harold Podd who was a fruitier. In the late 1930's the shop became Sylvia's wool shop and carried on into the late 1980's. Today in 2018 J. C. Marjoram & Co are operating as accountants.

No.488 in the 1930's Pierre Perredes opened his chemist shop and carried on until the 1940's when the shop passed to Jason Eccles, but by the 1950's David Morton had taken over.

In the 1957 phone book the shop was David Morton- Chemist & Photographic Dealer and he stayed well into the 1980's, but I remember this shop as a green grocers. Today in 2019 the shop appears just to be a private house.

No.490, London Road South.

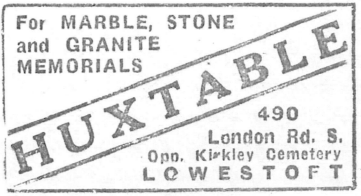

For MARBLE, STONE and GRANITE MEMORIALS

HUXTABLE

490 London Rd. S.
Opp. Kirkley Cemetery
LOWESTOFT

In 1909 this was the home and workshop of Mr Edwin Brown who as you can see was a monumental mason and he had a prime location dead opposite the front gates of Kirkley cemetery gates.

By the time the 1938 edition of Kelly Directory came out the business appears to have been taken over by Huxtable Monumental Masons, but today the area has been cleared and two terrace houses put up in its place.

No.496-498, London Road South.

Gwen Dolyn
HAIR STYLIST
496 London Rd. South, Lowestoft
For Next Appointment Tel. 5180

In 1909 No.496 was the private home of Thomas R Goldsmith and soon after converted to a shop where he set up a fishmongers. When the 1938 Kelly's came out the business had passed to Sydney Poole Jr who operated out of the building as a fruitier, but in the 1950's the shop changed ownership and became a boot repair shop by Thomas Thacker. In the 1960's the shop started its association with being a hairdressers, first with Gwen Dolyn, then Hair Affair and now in 2018 with being Ben Charles hair salon.

No.498 in 1909 was the home of a Mr Charles Goldsmith and by 1922 Louis Easey had set up shop as an ironmongers. It remained an ironmongers to well into the 1980's, first in 1925 when the business passed from Mr Easey to his wife Lucy and then to Horace Victor Wilson who carried on the business to the 1970's. In the phonebook for 1972 the business had passed to E. G. Pink and today the shop is knocked through into No.496.

No.558-560, London Road South.

These two shops started out as private houses and then shops and now back to houses or rather flats in the case of No.560. In 1909 No.558 was the home of Alan Soulter who operated out of the building as a dairy. It remained as a dairy right up to the 1950's, second with Mrs Grace Colby and then with Frederick Muddeman. In 1952 Frederick stopped the shop being a dairy and converted the shop into a café. Back in the 1990's a family friend Bob Storey used to own the Corton Hut and he would send me here Monday mornings to pick up that week's flyers for the nightclub Gators because it was Rapid Print.

In 1909 No.560 was the home of Charles William Wright who was a pork butchers, but by 1938 a Mr Harold Podd who also had a grocers at No.486 moved into the meat business. By the 1940's a Mr Poole had taken over and it became a green grocers right up to the 1970's when it then became Ann-Teak bric-a-brac shop. I remember it being first Speedy Tomatoes takeaway then another second-hand shop and now back to a private house.

No.564, London Road South.

Alfie and Margaret welcome you to

THE CARLTON

LONDON ROAD SOUTH, PAKEFIELD

Friday, 24th   DISCO BY 'JUDGE ONE'
Saturday, 25th   FANCY DRESS DISCO by 'IMPACT'

Open until 11.45.
Cheap drinks for those in fancy dress

Sunday, 26th   DISCO by 'IMPACT'
Tuesday 28th   SHOE SALE

Good quality fashion Lady's Sandals and Mules at
Knockdown Prices. All sizes and styles. **Starts 8 p.m.**

DISCO every Thursday by **"IMPACT"**
ALL FREE ENTERTAINMENT

The Carlton appeared in Kelly Directory in the 1922 edition with a John W Atkins as landlord. You can see from this advert from 1982 that Alfie and Margaret were landlord and landlady and they had a lot going on at the weekend at the Carlton. Today in 2018 the pub is as popular as ever and on its Facebook page it says; "Friendly local pub run by a local family." But the reviews speak for themselves. "Great live music from Annie & they sell Aspall cider so top marks for that. Clean, comfortable & friendly. It was our first visit and was pleasantly surprised. Why not check out the facebook page or better still visit the Carlton!

No.658, London Road South.

Well we have reached the end of our journey together along London Road South, the picture on the left is from the Robert Whybrow collection and was taken in the 1980's and you can see the first or last petrol station along London Road South depending which way you were travelling in the 1980's. Today in 2018 you cannot buy fuel anymore on the road and the Shell station has gone being replaced by houses. In 1972 listed in the Kelly Directory was Terminus Filling Station run by a Mr William G Cook, it was called Terminus Filling Station as from 1904 to 1931 this is where the trams used to terminate and then travel back North. Back in the 1930's the site stood empty, but a Mr John Day was in ownership of the land back in 1922.